Day of the
Border Guards

Day of the Border Guards

Poems by Katherine E. Young

The University of Arkansas Press
Fayetteville
2014

ISBN-10: 1-55728-655-8
ISBN-13: 978-1-55728-655-0

18 17 16 15 14   5 4 3 2 1

Text design by Ellen Beeler

♾ The paper used in this publication meets the minimum require-
ments of the American National Standard for Permanence of Paper
for Printed Library Materials Z39.48-1984.

Library of Congress Control Number: 2013953938

For Alexander, always.

Acknowledgments

Grateful acknowledgement is made to the editors of the following publications, in which some of these poems appeared in earlier form:

Archipelago: "Red Vineyard, 1888: A Painting by Van Gogh,"
   "The Arrest: May 13, 1934" (as "The Arrest")
The Carolina Quarterly: "Old Maps," "No Dog in This Fight,"
   "Nearing Chernobyl," "June Snow"
The Chattahoochee Review: "Centralized Heating," "Zagorsk"
The Delmarva Review: "Evdokia," "Kingdom of Heaven"
Gargoyle: "Fish Tale," "On the Bosphorus"
The Innisfree Poetry Journal: "Last Flight of the Gypsy King,"
   "Driving the M8"
The Iowa Review: "The Cow," "Wreaths," "Reading *Mr. Lincoln's
   Army*," "At the Lermontov Museum" (as "Lermontov's
   Room"), "Peredelkino"
The Massachusetts Review: "Lady Macbeth in the Caucasus"
Measure: "My KGB File"
Mount Hope: "Speaking English"
Naugatuck River Review: "City of Bells"
Terrain.org: "Day of the Border Guards," "Knitting in Siberia,"
   "Siberian Spring"

"Old Maps" was featured online by *Poetry Daily* on February 20, 1999.

"Nearing Chernobyl" was featured in Christopher Windolph's essay for *Spreading the Word: Editors on Poetry, Revised and Expanded Edition* (The Bench Press, 2001).

Earlier versions of some of these poems also appeared in the chapbook *Van Gogh in Moscow* (Pudding House Press, 2008).

Special thanks to Enid Shomer for believing in this collection and laboring over it. Thanks also to Greg McBride, Patric Pepper, Anne Harding Woodworth, and members of the Capitol Hill Poetry Group for seeing these poems through many iterations; to Karren Alenier and Miles David Moore for supporting the development of these poems; to Elizabeth Arnold, Pamela Harrison, Hailey Leithauser, Susan Mockler, Kurt Olsson, and Mary-Sherman Willis, who reviewed all or part of the manuscript at various stages; to my teachers and fellow students at the University of Maryland; to Alexander Woronzoff-Dashkoff and the late Nadezhda Yakovleva Mirova, who taught me about Russian poetry; and to John P. Williams, without whom this collection could not have been made.

Contents

III. Peredelkino   *45*

I.

Day of the
Border Guards

Old Maps

Rostov-on-Don, Russia

The river's the same, curving
gentle and infinite from right
to left across the frame.
And the street grid sketched out
in an age of absolutes,
it's still there—no one
would dream of changing it.
There's still a square
in the old town center,
and the cathedral's
ancient head has been fitted
with a new gold cap.
But factories have filled in
fields beyond the rails,
and the hippodrome
has shifted shape—if
you believe the maps—
from oval to rectangle.
What used to be the town
next door is now Our Town.
Soon Engels Street
will go back to being
Garden Street, I guess;
and Kirov's bust
(its nameplate comically
misspelled) will be leaving
the park. But they'll keep

the column that marks
the War, clumsy metal fins
still weighing down
its gilt star. A changeable
wind will still moan down
the streets—sharp-
tongued, implacable—
blowing the seasons
right out of town.

Reading *Mr. Lincoln's Army*

Sheremetyevo Airport, Moscow

Tonight I'm reading *Mr. Lincoln's Army*
in a holding cell near Sheremetyevo.

McClellan's writing to his Ellen of
the "original Gorilla" (he means Lincoln)—

Mac's been called upon to save the nation.
My watch shows 10 p.m., but I've flown

across the ocean, I'm in some nether hour.
Right now, it seems just as likely that I

could be that self-same Ellen—tight-corseted,
hooped, done up in sprigged muslin, reading

my lover's letter in the drawing room—
as myself, arriving late, without a visa.

I stir, shiver, touch my hand to the nightstand.
This cell resembles every room in Russia:

the same beige-papered walls, same tiles crumbling
in the bath, the same gray-flecked linoleum

ruching across the floor. Outside, my jailors
snore in their chairs. I maintain the fiction

that all's well this night: now I'm Little Mac
telling my Ellen how I'll save the country

from itself—*I'm not the type*, I say, to bolt
awake later, staring, astonished with fright.

Centralized Heating

At dawn the heat resumes its liquid journey
through iron casings bent like whalebone stays

to fit a waist of air. Over breakfast,
I read the death notices: *Died from burns*

incurred when ice gave way above a ruptured
pipe. And still they lay uninsulated

pipe, because that's what they've always done.
Whole neighborhoods, entire Russian cities

conjoin along these grids of heating lines,
hot-water mains: each year a few unlucky

souls tumble into their ancient workings, martyrs
to a theory that was never quite perfected.

Outside the clouds dribble pale gray snow;
I blow on my cold fingers, pressing them

to the radiator's ribs, just barely warm.
Across the way, a woman's used the tepid

water for her wash: wet bras and girdles,
lingerie, stretch rigid and plain along

her balcony. I hear the groan of water
gurgling through the pipes, the muffled squeal

of Moscow's thirteen million taps turning
in unison. What do we truly share,

this Russian washerwoman and I? Only
these iron heating veins, these leafless birches

shivering in the ice-covered courtyard.
A certain elasticity of mind:

the way we softly mouth the words *God rest
his soul* before we turn our thoughts away.

Speaking English

Sounds so cold—
like seasons growing old,
like late March snow
spitting at the sill
where an ill-used crow
gently mends rents
in wind-ravaged wings,
like shovels in savage song
rasping against asphalt—
sounds so crude
you can hear in them
bones straining to heft
the might of the universe.
Only the *o*—throaty,
unflinching—soars past
the clicking, grinning shears
and metal thickets poised
to clip back its solo.

Speaking Russian

When she saw the cat's ears, the vet blanched

Gololeditsa, naked ice. Nuts spill from cloth sacks

Mushrooms: forests to be gathered

casually, beside the burned-out tanks

In the early morning of the fourteenth day of the spring month of Nisan

greeted by cheering delegations of workers and
World War II veterans

women and children were thrown in the river

sleeves embroidered with seed pearls

Russian poetry died of self-consciousness in 1840

Wearing a stylish brown cloche in the sepia-toned photo

I take the trolley to the homeopathic pharmacy, clutching my

Fur hat? Genuine Red Army knife? Lacquer box?

Baidarka: two-man kayak

Machine-gunned, their bodies rolled down the ravine

black swans on a burdock-choked pond

So cold men's fingers froze

Blend almond oil with yellow dock root extract

I'm still unsure of instrumental plurals

The antechamber of learning is the knowledge of languages

the cat pays for my mistakes

Fish Tale

We no longer talk
of fallout shelters,
though the black-yellow
signs still hang
in stairwells back home;
why the Russians
would bomb Farmville
is still a mystery
to me. In Moscow, too,
the light poles still
sprout loudspeakers,
relics of that time:
at twilight their gap-
mouthed shadows
caress four small boys
who dangle the carcasses
of fish on strings,
inventing the lamplight,
the tin trumpets,
the trail of dusty,
iridescent fish scales
as they make
their way along.

Nearing Chernobyl

Summer 1987

Outside a village we stop by the road:
the air hangs pale, the gold-leaved birches
shiver dew from their fingers. The crust
of the earth breaks beneath my feet
as I pick out a path in the tentative way
that all cityfolk walk on unmown grass.
But there's tentative and tentative:
this morning I examine every blade,
every stalk, jump at each crackle of
the shifting frost, fear that enchantment
will steal over me. As if enchantment
can be scented on the wind, or tasted
in a gooseberry. As if it rides on the backs
of the men plowing fields there,
beyond the trees; or rises, steaming,
from this tree root where I crouch, concealed.
Perhaps I shouldn't touch the tree's bole,
the long grass; perhaps then it will pass me by,
as in a fairy tale whose heroine wears
an invisible ring to wander unscathed
through Death's portal and back.
For there's enchantment aplenty here:
the cold wheeling of comets, breath
of the sun howling down on the rump
of a woman peeing by a tree in Ukraine.
I carry the dust of the universe on my shoes.

The Cow

The road from Samarkand
slices blue-black and bored
through the salt-veined desert,
past cotton fields bleached
copper green and white,
past mulberries massed
in dusty ranks like soldiers
of the Great Khan. Leaving
town, we thread our way
through busloads of women
and children bound for those fields,
a "voluntary" Sunday
picking cotton. It's November:
clear and cold. We woke
in pre-dawn darkness—the stars
of Ulug Beg wheeling
about the astringent heavens—
dressed ourselves in silence,
fingers thick with chill.
Snorting, bucking, the bus
complains its way forward,
exhaling little puffs
of air perfumed with lemon
disinfectant. We day-
dream caravans of hard-
mouthed camels, salve imagined
saddle sores, brush

the coruscating sand
from flesh etched by desert
winds. Cross-pollinating
cultures—Mongol faces
girding Russian churches,
a verb meaning *the ground
reddens with blood*, the harem
of the last Bukhara emir
"rescued" by Red Army
regulars (they tell us
the ladies went willingly)—
the desert pays no heed,
puzzling only now
and then at the asphalt
ribbons unfurling among
its oases. Here, in the careless
way of deserts and seas,
it casts up a peril:
groan. Shudder. Halt.
Throaty Uzbek vowels:
Flat tire. Please to walk out.
We stumble onto sculpted
sand, follow the sun
as it creeps cautiously
along the ridge, fingers
the horns of a solitary
cow: head tipped back,
legs collapsed beneath,
eyes run wild in sudden,
staggering intimation
of what it means to be
mortal. *Been dead some time*,
opines a man, surveying
the carcass with a practiced

air. He spits, satisfied,
as if he's just divined
some mystery. The crowd
breaks into twos and threes,
some wandering up the nearest
slope, some clumping close
to where the driver, grunting,
wrestles a tire to the axle.
Back on the bus, we rummage
for water, snacks, guidebooks
among our day-glo packs,
bags stuffed with prayer rugs,
embroidered hats, *suzani*.
My neighbor settles a sweater
about her shoulders to nap.
The bus follows the road,
the road follows the sand,
the sand runs unchanging
to Bukhara, looped and laced
by a veil of frailest green:
too frail to sanctify
a dead cow kneeling in dust,
bemused stars—nothing—
reflected in her eyes.

Lady Macbeth in the Caucasus

Were such things here as we speak about?
Or have we eaten on the insane root
That takes the reason prisoner?
                    —Act I, Scene 3, 83–85

Here in the mountains, it's the same old plot:
the swearing of oaths, laying of snares, some
modern-day Lady Macbeth checking voicemail.
Thus begins the hurly-burly. No spurious
tartan nailed to this crag, this sharp-boned, sheep-clad
shoulder of the world—even the clouds
drift murderous here. From a nearby church spills
the pink-gray scent of sheep guts and sour wine.
Still, the waters run clear, and the barbed-wire
stars shine fixed, unwinking, girding the heavens
in their steely embrace. All hangs in the balance
while she pauses the tape—hearing, perhaps,
the merest betraying tremor in his voice—
and, frowning, saves the message, to listen to later.

No Dog in This Fight

Chechnya, 1995

In the video passed from hand to hand,
we see what's coming: thugs in boots
shoot off their Uzis, dance the *dhikr*
before Dudayev, who applauds
from the palace roof in his uniform
of azure blue. Women chant
the ninety-nine names of God
in ululating circles now
coalescing, now dissolving
in the earthen square beneath. Who
can read these people, fathom their ways?
How can a Samaritan give aid?
The weak will die, they always do:
at Samashki, Russians get high,
take turns at raping Chechen women
and kids before they shoot them dead;
in Grozny, starving Russian grannies
prowl the ruins in search of rats.
Refugees pack the border towns,
shoving among lone women seeking
their sons. The conscripts tell this story:
rockets screaming, mortars pounding,
a woman comes from out of nowhere,
marches right up to the lieutenant
colonel, she says, *You come home, son,*
and off they go, as if there weren't
a battle going on. As if

nothing mattered in the whole wide
world except their own two selves.
What gives a man courage in places
like these? Back home, this stuff won't make
the evening news, an internal Russian
affair: *ain't got no dog in this fight.*
And to the stranger bringing succor
in this squalid little war, is it
much comfort, thinking he'll go home
to a land of self-evident truths,
to hot and cold running water,
to all-night diners? He's a large-
boned man; they'll find remains.

Frederick C. Cuny, in memoriam

Wreaths

*Ring Road, Moscow, on the fiftieth anniversary of the
liberation of Auschwitz*

While wreaths are laid and speeches made
and statesmen find their photo ops
in shrieking lights at the Wall of Death,
a man staggers out through seven
lanes of traffic to the center
of the road, dead center. And if
he stretches out his hands, his fingers
will touch the chrome and magic before
being torn off. Some secret grief
makes him fall to his knees, swaying
gently, gently. But who has a soul
so great it holds all the world within?
Behind their windows, drivers stare
and honk at him. I press my palm
to the glass of the tram before moving on.

Day of the Border Guards

May 29, 1987: German Teen Lands Plane in Red Square

This story's true: spring at last in Moscow,
time of thawing earth, of drying mud.
Sunshine and mist hopscotch across Red Square:
stones the color of smoke, St. Basil's domes,
those child-sized Kremlin windows. Banners flutter
from lampposts to proclaim today the Day
of the Border Guards; in front of Lenin's Tomb,
young border guards in parade regalia snap
photographs, some laughing, some tugging
girls by the hand, some already draped
across the shoulders of their comrades. Except
for the clothes, the cameras, today could be
any spring day in a thousand-year span:
I could be myself, or any one
of Pushkin's women, or Margarita walking
the alleys with yellow flowers in her arms.
So many possibilities: a man
I've never met spots my flowers, knows
immediately he's loved me all his life.
Onegin shouts at his coachman to stop.
I marry a general; I marry a madman.
I become a witch, an Old Believer,
a Streltsy wife sledging to Siberia.
Perhaps I poison myself—arsenic? Hemlock?
As I'm calculating the fatal dose,
a silvery object darts from the western sky:
I watch it circle, descend, buzz Red Square.

Someone shouts, *He's landing!* People start
pushing, running to get out of the way—
the airplane noses down at the southern edge
of Red Square. The young pilot—he can't be more
than seventeen—climbs out, extends his hand.
No one around me moves; I hold my breath.
And now an officer of the Border Guards
threads his way among the crowd, swaying
ever so gently across the sharp-edged stones.
Soon a thousand things will happen at once:
someone will shove a camera in my hand,
ask me to take his picture with the pilot.
Warning sirens will blare from the Kremlin.
Special Forces cops will swarm the plane:
they'll handcuff the boy, cordon off Red Square.
I'll be herded to the metro, lose
my flowers in the crush. Wonder what
it was I saw. Because now I'm a witness,
I stand and watch—we all watch—as slowly,
shockingly—that drunken officer
of the Border Guards stretches out ten trembling
fingers to print the faintest stain of hope
on the airplane's shiny metal skin.

for Barbara Roesmann

II.

Knitting in Siberia

Siberian Spring

Tomsk, Siberia

A moment for a painting: crisp, clean
snow sparking over hill and hollow,
barest green halo hovering above branches.
Taiga: the word smells fresh, unstained.
Gone are the long nights—woman, bottle, knife,
each good company in her own way—
swept clear by green noise.

Up front the driver tightens a wire in the engine.
Satisfying, these small victories:
the engine's rev, the road's drag,
the marking of another spring—
as if it were an easy thing.
As if any of it were easy.
Just ask the river ice, keening now
over the carcass of her rank,
disemboweled self.

Driving the M8

There are bandits on this road, the kind
who years ago would've lurked on horseback here
at forest's eave where the highway narrows
obligingly at the edge of Vladimir *oblast'*:
good spot for an ambush. I'm the one driving
in this dream, although in life you usually drive
the second-hand car with screw holes in the hood
and trunk where someone filched the BMW
emblems from right under the nose of the *dvornik*
who loiters all day in the parking lot, keeping
an eye on us foreigners (Whose eye? Why?).
Our car's muscular, smooth, but not like what
the bandits drive, those tint-windowed Mercedes
purring along the road, stiff-arming Soviet
models that run on rubber bands and spit.
Every Russian fixes cars. Sometimes
the BMW breaks down: I pop the hood,
make a show of feminine helplessness
for ten, fifteen seconds, till the screech
of tires, sometimes two or three sets, as the drivers
of Ladas or Zhigulis or—once—a Chaika
spring from their seats, wrenches in hand, itching
to take a look beneath that foreign hood.
They always manage to get it going again.

Now bandits broker the trade in beach towels—
hundreds of miles from the ocean, Mickey Mouse

waves his mitts from every clothesline an hour's
drive on either side of Sergiev Posad.
We ask ourselves what the profit is in that
but can't come up with a satisfactory answer.
Oh, you're here—funny, I left alone. . . .
Look! There's a bandit pulling off the road.
Cigarette dangling, Ray Bans cocked, he's young,
smooth-shaven, with something slightly vulpine about
his cheek and nascent jowl. The kind of man
who rarely looks at me, which is best
because one glance in those ferocious, needy
eyes and I'm a goner, I'm mom and whore
and Little Red Riding Hood all rolled into one.
The bandit bends to flick mud from his shoe
as he shakes down the owners of beat-up cars
parked by the roadside, impromptu market
in enamel pans, patterned curtains, crystal
chandeliers: opportunity knocking.

I take it back: you're not in this dream, after all.
You're never in my dreams anymore. Twenty-
five years of tuna melts, nylon sheers,
utility bills, and suddenly you've vanished,
poof! As if you'd never been. As if
you hadn't dragged the mattress across the room
on our wedding night, although it was one hundred
and ten in the dark and the tiny window a/c
might as well have been broken. As if
you hadn't wept next morning when you posed
among bouquets and empty champagne bottles
for the photograph still propped beside my bed:
proof that joy exists, in spite of all
our dreary evidence to the contrary.
No matter: I'm following the wolf pack now,

I'm on the scent of danger. I know full well
there's a dumpster in my future, only,
god, not today, oh, not today. Today
I'm driving on what passes for a highway
in Russia and, instead of you, maybe
my passenger's a highwayman: yes.
Maybe I'm driving him along his rounds.
You're beautiful, he says in his Russian way,
stroking my cheek and blowing smoke out the window.
Or maybe I'm the one who's saying it,
because it's true—he's beautiful as wild,
beautiful as feral, beautiful
as fear. Soon we're stopping at a hamlet
composed of a dozen knock-kneed cottages.
My bandit's all business counting out
his cut from jars of fresh pickles, pails
of potatoes, buckets of cut daisies clustered
at the feet of an empty stool that leans
against a half-hinged gate. I'm tasting one
of those pickles, feather-frond of dill
still clinging to its rind, swallowing
the brine and gall of being ornamental.
Serviceable. I've decided there's no
such thing as essential: we're—all of us—
intimate strangers who'll disappear some morning:
tomorrow, or next month, or maybe twenty-
five years along the line, joy becoming
theoretical as it vanishes, unbelief
chafing fingers where rings once held sway.

With bandits, at least, I know what I'm getting.
My passenger's eyes stray to the gate, where
a blonde, lipsticked siren accidentally
hooks her miniskirt as she hastens to meet us.

Underwear flashes pink: pattern of hearts.
This village lies at the end of the universe.
I know what's coming next: my tongue is
torn out. I change myself to a nightingale.
Now, too late, you come looking for me.
You recognize the place: storks nesting in chimneys,
scrollwork edging the windows, scent of onions
and mushrooms infusing the air. All
the cottages sag in unison toward a church
whose star-speckled dome has split in two.

for John

The Parrot Flaubert

That spring she couldn't rid herself of him:
his essence lingered in the rows of boxwood,
the balky lawn mower, the wheelbarrow
with the flat tire he'd propped against the porch.
Magazines, bills kept coming in his name.
Ants still overran the pantry, bait
untouched, as if she'd never set it out.
She had to remind herself he'd really gone.
Those last months he'd sequestered himself
in the basement, flitting from channel to channel,
crowds of celluloid Welleses and Garbos
repelling all her efforts to engage him.
Unhappiness sprouted thorns, muscled in
among the end tables. The words of a Russian
cabaret song lodged in her brain, evoking
fine china, Chantilly spoons, hand-knotted rugs.
She recalled the stillness in which he'd sat—
he'd seemed impervious—while the final
verse played out around him: the once-plucky
heroine, driven to hysterics, smashing
plates; the old cat saucer-eyed beneath
the sofa; and the parrot Flaubert, sobbing
uncontrollably again *en français.*

June Snow

Snatches of *Carmen* whistle through windows;
gossamer fibers filter the light.

Objects appear through a web wrought so spare
it twines unnoticed round the throat

caught unaware. So it is with the selves
I've shed, met suddenly in the metro,

brushing *pukh* from my clothes—outrush of breath—
chance, absolute, irrevocable.

And blown on that finite, expiring sigh, the ghost
of you—random, evanescent

as seed from the lovelorn poplar spinning in piles
while boys wait, cradling matches, nearby.

for Christopher

Yellow Flowers

After Mikhail Bulgakov

I buttoned my long black coat, settled
yellow flowers in my arms,
struck out along Tverskaya, scanning
the shop windows, the faces, the cars:

it was either that, or poison myself.
I'd never met you—I'd known you all
my life. I turned down an alley
the moment I saw you. You knew me, too:

we met, as if by chance, among
dumpsters and coal chutes. You liked
roses, you said, but not these flowers—
Yellow's an evil color, you said.

Love caught us suddenly, leaped
at us like a murderer. I tossed
my yellow signal in the gutter,
tucked my hand beneath your arm.

Names for Snow

There are hundreds of names for snow, you say,
unlatching the *fortochka* in morning light.
Let's name them all, love, along the way.

Last night snow danced its boreal ballet
of whorls and swirls, fine arabesques in white—
you know hundreds of names for snow, you say.

Down crystalline paths we slip and spin, surveying
ice falls, tall drifts, single flakes in flight—
my love and I count them along the way.

In my head, sparkling visions start to play:
once love's begun, who knows? Perhaps we might—
There are hundreds of names for snow, you say,

gently, *their meanings subtle, hard to convey—*
elusive as love's many meanings last night.
I wait. You walk—silent—along your way.

Feeling foolish, unschooled, I whisk away
a sudden, childish tear obscuring my sight.
You know hundreds of names for love, you say:
I'll learn them all, love, along my way.

Last Flight of the Gypsy King

Tomsk Airport, Siberia

Gypsies' cries engulf the hall:
their black-eyed king has died too young.
Overdose, the desk clerk says.
He shakes his head, tearing my ticket
with inky fingers. The gypsy king
requires a ticket, too, his body
charged as cargo, counted among
the crates, hand-tagged for destination.

> *Last night I drank with the gypsy king.*
> *He offered me pearls and precious things.*
> *We drank to friendship, love, and art;*
> *he gave me dewdrops from his heart.*

In the lounge, we women secure bags
beneath our arms as we pause before
the mirror, glancing nervously
at a gypsy girl who lifts her hem
to wipe wet eyes. Everyone fears
the gypsies' light-fingered ways:
peddlers of dross, crocodile tears,
traffickers in our secret dreams.

> *Last night I danced with the gypsy king;*
> *we danced, forgetting everything,*
> *his arms around me strong and warm,*
> *his kinglets sleeping back at home.*

Gypsies mill around the gate
jostling against the passengers,
tearing their hair, clinging to one
another. The dead king's children, dressed
in velvet, pass from hand to hand
like glass-eyed dolls. Their mother wails
as if her heart might break. As if
no one had ever died before.

Last night I lay with the gypsy king,
his hands upon me trembling.
We lay, and loved, until the dawn,
until his wife came calling, calling. . . .

for Elizabeth Miles

City of Bells

How can it matter in what tongue I
Am misunderstood by whomever I meet. . . .
                   —Marina Tsvetaeva

The songs of my life collect in trams, smelling
of cabbage and stale smoke and yesterday's
night out. Their melodies orbit the city,
resonate in half-lives—murmurs, grunts,
the thin whine of excuse—cacophony
of a cockeyed city where hammers ring
in resurrected belfries and motors whir
in the Savior's Tower to synchronize the chimes.

Nothing harrows the wounded soul like music
that takes it unaware: click and trill
of English overheard along Arbat,
careless peal of long-tongueless bells,
swirling cry of a of blue-hooded crow
that falls and rises like a heartbeat. I know
exactly what you mean, Marina: it doesn't
matter where I'm altogether lonely.

Here in your beloved city, autumn
frost incises the leaves: season for pickling
mushrooms, for rowanberry jam. For regrets.
Unlike yours, my exile's voluntary—
what I call *home* is neither here nor there.
I drift from hand to hand, tongue to tongue,
tuning my ear to the one disfigured note,
the too-regular breath, the broken spell.

My lover's gone, Marina: his words scatter
like birch leaves in the snow. Now he lives
with an ordinary woman. He's turned his back
on the gods with their nimble-fingered fluting,
spits *fthip-fthip-fthip* to keep evil at bay.
No one now will pause to recall the rhymes
of his life or the sound of his singing:
drone of a fly on the face of dank earth.

What's Left

Only the murmur of gathering snow,
and, far off, the squeal of teeth

shearing steel, and the ashy scent
of solder riding the air; only

the blue-hooded crow, scolding
from an archway at us below;

only the thin-lipped solstice sun,
glancing anxiously across

your shoulder as you turn away;
only your voice, too faint for an echo:

How fine you are! Only turnstile,
platform, tracks seaming sudden fractures

in the earth; only this seat astride
my suitcase, train hastening on.

Knitting in Siberia

Let me warn you that a genuine interest in knitting can keep you fascinated, eagerly pursuing it, and never satisfied, through a lifetime.

—Rose Wilder Lane, *The Woman's Day
Book of American Needlework*

i.

I've been thinking about the prairie, Rose,
how that word means the same in every language.
This prairie sweeps out east, not west, but speaks—
like all prairies—of freedom and fair chance.
It's April in Siberia: dodging
drops from gables, eaves, rickrack bedecking
the city's wooden homes, I hear ice blocks
shudder, heave, as the river wrenches free.
Tomsk, too, was once a prairie town like all
the little towns in your mother's books, books
girls like me still use to gauge our childhood.
Imagine my surprise to find you here
in grown up life, you chaperoning Laura
in the Gold Rush city to which you'd run,
mother and daughter already colluding in
one another's fictions: *I do want
to do a little writing with Rose to get
the hang of it a little better so I
can write something perhaps I can sell.*
As good a plan as any. How things get started.

ii.

I've flown across the Urals, needles clicking
through the Russian sky. This morning I met
with modern-day homesteaders who'll hawk
their business plans in America. Like
our ancestors, Rose, they're a motley crew:
the naïve young mountaineer who's engineered
new climbing gear; the ex-KGB hack,
mouth full of golden teeth, who waves a letter
from the region's governor; the woman
crafting an empire of cigarette kiosks.
Why does hope always lie over yonder,
in a place someone else has left behind?
Tonight, in my hotel on this strange prairie,
I'll look at stars, their unfamiliar postings;
I'll think of sledges packed with Old Believers,
women and children shivering across
the permafrost. Of the wagon your mother rode
to Kansas, Minnesota, and beyond,
kettle and washboard rattling in the back,
Jack the bulldog trotting along beside.
No turning back, not then. No second thoughts.

iii.

Here's what I know: point of the needle jabbing
my finger, snarl of yarn, reel and loop,
the tying off of stitches. Rose, you taught me
how to knit when my own mother gave up:
she blamed it on my left hand, said she couldn't
teach me backwards. . . . It's not my mother, Rose,
nor any man, nor any dream that's gone
awry: just the need to see what's out here,
find what sort of place might be my own.
Home's folded in a suitcase, hand-cabled
in a sweater: what I carry in my pack.
Phone calls from my mother—that singular ring
the phone makes when the call's from overseas—
I learn that someone's died, that someone's
been born just from the way she says *Hello?*
Tangle of wire, switches, satellite dishes:
the knots with which we bind ourselves.
I thread over my needle, purl a new row
in the baby blanket I'm knitting for a nephew
I've never seen back there in America.
I parse each stitch backwards, steadying
the yarn as it slackens, twists free and, then,
pulls taut: same pattern that our mothers picked out.
That we teach ourselves. Repeat.

Kingdom of Heaven

Novodevichy Convent, Moscow, sixteenth century

i.

At thirteen, I learned to be a woman:
to limn my skin with lead, like snow,

to brush my brows with antimony,
shape and shade of a sable's tail.

To rouge my cheeks with beets until
they gleamed like poppies, pull back

my hair so tight I feared I'd faint:
not one single strand could show.

To dilate my pupils with stinging
drops so my eyes would catch the light

just like a falcon's. I was lucky:
a man saw I was beautiful—

saw I was strong. But he himself
was weak: he died before our wedding.

ii.

Now I pass my days embroidering faces,
studding the halos of saints with pearls.
Fishbone, feather stitch, chain and tuck:
I work their flesh in peach-tongued silk.

iii.

Sometimes in dreams I walk a path
where gold-leaved birches rustle and nod
against an autumn sky. Mushrooms

cluster at the roots of trees, poppies
spill their seed on the fields. I sniff—listen—
my hair, my body now unbound. The path

is peopled with creatures: beneath dry,
dusky skin, the earth stirs, whispers
the language of our feet. In this dream,

my fur glows richer than the sable's.
I am flying with the falcon.
I am snowing perfect pearls.

III.

Peredelkino

On the Bosphorus

Call me *effendi*. I've crossed over seas
to drowse here on your shore like new-formed dew.
Ports of call are mostly the same, differing
just in disposition of souls, in name,
in degree of grizzle betokening wisdom.
And in fear, attuned to climate, current,
and the frequency of pirates appearing
in these parts. I'm something of a pirate
myself—in landfalls and sirens' calls
I reckon my wealth, though any reckoning's
subjective: where some see sirens, others see
sea cows (I've catholic tastes, nominally
discriminate). You've a fine wharf here,
a princely trade in boats, their muscular holds
laden with Black Sea booty. From the empty
terminal—its turnstile leading nowhere,
leading everywhere—I watch the ferryman's
daughter enchain a flower in her hair.

Joseph Brodsky, in memoriam

At the Lermontov Museum

The hollow heart beats evenly.
—Mikhail Lermontov

He himself would have hurried up
these breakneck stairs, along this hall,
boot heels clack-clacking to the rat-
tat-tat of *grand-maman*'s disapproval.
It's a familiar story, the old
and the young: she thinking he won't
amount to much if he doesn't
shape up, he believing she just
doesn't get what life's about. . . .
His aerie's here, atop the house,
conjured out of November cloud.
A poet's place: Pushkin above
the desk; the peaks of the Caucasus
engraved, fantastic; leather-bound
Byrons, Schillers, and Chéniers
spilling cockeyed across the shelves.
Ask the *dezhurnaya* who sits
by the door and she'll recite his verses,
rocking gently with the rhythm,
thinking back to those days at school
when it had seemed to her the most
romantic thing, to die young.

My KGB File

Notes from 1981

My folder's slim, tied shut with string: flaps
at top and bottom guard against stray slips
of paper. I'd imagined what I'd find
within, the pages acid-yellow, fading:
Met Subject—meaning me—*in Sverdlov Square*
(he didn't report the pocket calculator
I'd smuggled him from his sister in L.A.).
Subject seen sketching the Lenin Hills Bridge
(unexpected handwritten addendum:
I was almost arrested!). *Subject raised toasts*
to fraternity among peoples (can this
be you, dear Lena, informing on me?)
Next, photos: *Subject riding the tram*, buying
plums at the market, sampling *pirozhki*
near the Pushkin Museum. Nothing untoward,
unplanned-for, nothing out of the ordinary.
Subject shows scant interest in our so-
called "dissidents." Here a question mark's
penciled in the margin. There are two
likely answers, each equally unsettling:
Subject—meaning me—saw, but felt nothing;
Subject—meaning me—was unable to see.

Pushkin Museum of Fine Arts

But how little they resembled the gods
who wore winged crowns in allegorical paintings,
those dissidents who frowned through scotch-taped glasses
and shook their fingers at my naïveté.
No more than I resembled Icarus
falling from the sky, my failures even
more ordinary. What amazed me then:
the armies of the everyday who woke
each morning and set patiently about
making something of their lives, despite
every conceivable incentive to do
nothing. Onetime ploughmen throttled combines,
the torturer's chauffeur strained his back
changing a flat, printers inked metal plates
to print the newspapers office workers
used to wrap up fish. On the *Koltso*,
trucks belched smoke; and up in space men floated
in expensive delicate ships and watched
the earth in blue radiance whirling away.

Thirty Years Later

Evening and snow: the bus draws
a line feathered in lead, the forest
flickers with indifferent flakes.
The season feels fresh, forgiving.

Behind us, now, the stone-toothed hills,
the broken-back churches, convents
and stations where women were shorn:
all safely behind, all shriven.

Before us the city, white licking
the brick, the stone shoulders, lips
stiffened to bronze—and Volodya
Kornilov, back bent in sentence,

clearing snow from the pavement.
Why couldn't I see? All my life,
I've plied the sidelines, doubting idols,
seeking out frauds: the *fartsovchik*

dealing icons for jeans, the girl
trading friendship for my winter
coat, the boy who flirted and smirked,
wanting to meet somewhere just

us two. I've believed in no one—
everyday saints were alien

to me. Volodya, you know better
than most how long it takes to nourish

a soul: seed languishing in wintry
soil, sprouting in secret, thrusting up
a new, green shoot when least expected.
Sometimes it takes thirty years:

snow spattering the windshield, shovel
scraping the curb, papery rasp
of a workman's song, crisp, visible,
suspended in the freezing air.

Vladimir Kornilov, in memoriam

Red Vineyard, 1888: A Painting by Van Gogh

If I ever get back, the first thing I shall do is go and see the
French [paintings].

—Osip Mandelstam in exile

I still remember his vermilion, color
with the grandest name—it tasted of tree trunks,
a workman's blouse, the sugar-sharp grapes
ripe for harvest in the vineyards of Arles.
He'd captured the sun and hung it—toasted gold
like *blini* hot, hot from the stove—to wester
there beyond the fields. *What gives life*
is incomparable: and though my path now lies
through the transit camps, along *Vtoraya rechka*,
I float on the arc of unbeginning journeys.
Pity, instead, the man who surveyed this spot,
forced to reduce the vast East to a chart,
chilled fingers inking, there, *First Little Stream*
and, there, *Third Little Stream*—equally soulless
names for places men are sent to die.
Understand this: there's no other road,
no roundabout crossing, no safer way.
There's Death, too, in that sunset—but not yet.
On the wet-black walk, chalk soil softly dusts
the blush and flutter of a sap-swollen bud.

The Arrest: May 13, 1934

I showed M[andelstam] a picture of a couple of extinct
parakeets, and he thought they looked very much like us.
                                    —*Nadezhda Mandelstam*

Above the chairs, a circle of light:
clink of spoons on borrowed plates.
A single, precious egg scavenged
for Anna nestles in its bowl.

Anna has come at M's request.
She smells of cigarettes, of damp
wool, of comfort. M's called to the phone:
the line clicks, clicks, disconnects.

Nadya pours tea, thinks, *How long*
will this take? Her hand shakes,
spilling fragrant drops on the photo
of Anna's son, who smiles shyly,

like the ghost of past lovers:
M's, or Anna's, or her own,
all jumbling together on this night
when booted strangers will rifle

the secrets of three lives. The talk
crawls on: M tells again how
he slapped Alexei Tolstoy's face.
Someone recites lines from Polonsky.

Nadya waits in the kitchen, measures
time as smoke enters, exits her lungs:
breathe, breathe. At one, the sharp, explicit
knock. She rises. Sits back down.

Evdokia

Peter the Great's first wife, from her nunnery

I fell silent. *Awake!* cried the sunshine
and daisies and milkweed so fine
and ephemeral. *Awake!* cried the wild crow,
fluttering covetous and low
above the corn. *Awake!* cried the grey mouse
sorting grain in his winter house
within my wall. *Awake!* cried the black monk
from inside of God's own great house.
And at his command I opened my mouth—
but they had torn out my tongue.

The Percussive Quality of Light

June 1993

The earth begins to breathe again.
Twilight mottles the hands of a woman
reclining in a book-lined alcove,
shelves crammed with photos, thick-spined journals,
African masks. Proffering tea
and homemade jam, she recollects
the time Nadezhda Mandelstam
brought her husband new, warm boots.
Back then we whispered forbidden verses—
that's how he wooed me, she confides.
Nights like this they'd walk and talk
along Patriarch's Pond—one met
everyone there. Imagine: click
and whistle of the mating call,
illicit rhythms masquerading
as footfalls, petty treasons concealed
by the crowds, leaves, the filaments
of *pukh* festooning the pebble path.

The more one loves, the more's to lose:
no wonder, then, in times of trouble
wise hearts slink down the nearest drain.
Those days, it seemed the hearts of Moscow
clustered like diamonds in metro tunnels,
waiting to be mined by the few
holy fools who weren't afraid
to smile at strangers riding the train.

Hearts flickered in the ring of gas
where a kettle steamed, tinkled against
the paper-thin rims of tea glasses,
dissolved into desire—*if only,*
if only—while their erstwhile possessors
shrugged their shoulders, shifting the load.
Later, the one who'd laughed loudest
dreamed of exploding suns, light
stabbing through keyholes, flinging open
long-closed cupboards, flushing its prey.

Nothing's turned out the way we'd hoped—
no lustration, no truth commission.
The old informants lounge in silk;
their girlfriends accessorize the bath.
The light that figured in all our dreams
proved puny, dull, its purifying
power just an old wives' tale.
Daylight fades across the relics,
testaments to a touching faith:
paintings eschewing official style,
books inscribed by vanished poets,
boots peeking out from beneath the coats.
The air burrs with the murmurings
of untamed minds. Scattered around
the room, spilling from ledges, tables,
the narrow sill: buds, sprays, bouquets
of dead flowers, left dangling in
their vases now the water's all gone.

Zagorsk

Sergiev-Posad Monastery

Happy endings look like this:
onions regilded, relics restored,
the pathway to Hell recartooned
on the wall. Even the tongues of the bells—
newly hung—whisper, *Redemption.*

Babas bustle among the tourists
snuffing out low-burning wicks;
smoke rises to wreath the cupola—
its whitewash gone—where God's come home,
luxuriant beard fresh-curled and combed.

The icons won their guerilla war:
these days they gaze indulgently
on cups, jars, jugs, plastic mouths
chivvied up to the spout from which
new miracles are said to spill.

Not like that other monastery
where workmen troll for tips giving
private tours of the burial pits,
where the river brushes past
bones that gnaw at the upturned earth.

Perhaps only one who's struck down
his own son can take the measure
of this land; perhaps the land hews men
in its image—ax, knout, flail—each wound
a beginning, each beginning a wound.

Peredelkino

Just look for two tall pines, we were advised,
but we missed the pines, feet turning over
dead leaves and creeping weeds as we combed
the iron grilles, the mounds blistering
the skin of the hill. An ancient need drove us,
as if the essence of the man might lie
there in the ground, rise tangible, reassuring,
to meet our idiot gaze: as if his snap
and whistle birdsong weren't enough. His stone,
when we found it, gave nothing away, the face—
intaglioed—inscrutable as a hieroglyph.
The sun set copper in an onion dome;
birches wrapped in paper rustled their leaves;
nearby, a nightingale began to sing.

Notes

"No Dog in This Fight"
Frederick C. Cuny was the American foreign-aid dynamo
abducted and killed in Chechnya during the early days of that
war. Cuny included the story of the lieutenant colonel and his
mother in "Killing Chechnya," an April 1995 article he wrote
for *The New York Review of Books*. The poem's title comes from
remarks in 1989 by then-US secretary of state James Baker
summarizing the American position on the conflict in the
Balkans, a war in which Cuny won international acclaim for
rendering humanitarian aid.

"Day of the Border Guards"
The Old Believers left the Russian Orthodox Church after the
seventeenth-century reforms of Patriarch Nikon; many were
exiled to Siberia. They continued (and continue) to worship
according to older practices and were persecuted for their
beliefs into the twentieth century.

"The Parrot Flaubert"
The song "The Parrot Flaubert" (1916), written by Russian
singer Alexander Vertinsky, details a romantic breakup
witnessed by a parrot belonging to one of the lovers. The song
ends with the parrot, Flaubert, sadly repeating "*Jamais, jamais*"
and weeping "in French."

"June Snow"
Pukh is the silky, fibrous coating of the seed produced by the
cottonwood tree, which was over-planted in Moscow following
the Second World War.

"Yellow Flowers"
In Mikhail Bulgakov's *The Master and Margarita*, Margarita abandons a sterile marriage for love of the Master.

"Names for Snow"
The *fortochka* is a small, latched window cut into a larger window that can be opened independently for ventilation.

"City of Bells"
The epigraph is from Elaine Feinstein's translation of "Homesickness."

"Knitting in Siberia"
Laura Ingalls Wilder's words are from a 1915 letter to Almanzo Wilder.

"At the Lermontov Museum"
Russian poet Mikhail Lermontov (1814–1841), a younger contemporary and admirer of Alexander Pushkin, is considered second only to Pushkin in his artistry. Like Pushkin, he died very young, in a duel. In Russian museums, older women are often employed as a *dezhurnaya*, a cross between museum guard and docent.

"Thirty Years Later"
In his poem "Forty Years Later," Soviet poet Vladimir Kornilov alludes to the widely believed story that banned writer Andrei Platonov was employed as a janitor. Kornilov himself was forced to work for a short time as a street cleaner because of his dissident activities.

"*Red Vineyard, 1888:* A Painting by Van Gogh"
Vtoraya rechka, "Second Little Stream," is the transit camp where Mandelstam is believed to have perished. Mandelstam

reportedly composed his poetry to the rhythm of his own footsteps; the italicized phrases are from his poem "Don't compare: what gives life is incomparable."

"The Arrest: May 13, 1934"
On the night of Mandelstam's first arrest, poet Anna Akhmatova was staying with the Mandelstams.

"Zagorsk"
Pilgrims to Sergiev-Posad often bring containers from home to collect water from holy springs located on the monastery grounds.

Both Ivan IV (the Terrible) and Peter I (the Great) lost their eldest sons to court intrigue; neither son reigned after the father. Ivan's death led to a long period of instability, the Time of Troubles, that eventually brought the Romanov family to the throne.

"Peredelkino"
Peredelkino is the Moscow suburb and writer's colony where Boris Pasternak lived in his later years and is buried.